FEATHER AND BONE

Ruth Carr

FEATHER AND BONE

poems in response to
Dorothy Wordsworth (1771–1855)
Mary Ann McCracken (1770–1866)

ARLEN
HOUSE

Feather and Bone

is published in 2018 by
ARLEN HOUSE
42 Grange Abbey Road
Baldoyle, Dublin 13, Ireland
Phone: 00 353 85 7695597
arlenhouse@gmail.com
arlenhouse.blogspot.com

Distributed internationally by
SYRACUSE UNIVERSITY PRESS
621 Skytop Road, Suite 110
Syracuse, NY 13244–5290
Phone: 315–443–5534
Fax: 315–443–5545
supress@syr.edu
syracuseuniversitypress.syr.edu

978–1–85132–185–8, *paperback*
978–1–85132–186–5, *limited edition, signed and numbered hardback*

cover image by Daniela Balmaverde
is reproduced courtesy of the artist

CONTENTS

The hand was fire and the page tinder
Eavan Boland, 'The Lost Art of Letter Writing'

Mary Ann McCracken and Dorothy Wordsworth were born within a year of one another. Their paths never crossed. Mary Ann lived all her life among her family in Belfast, travelling to Dublin on drapery business as well as to visit her brothers when they were held in Kilmainham Gaol. Dorothy became an orphan in her early years and shifted from Cumbria to Yorkshire and eventually, after Alfoxden, back to the Lake District, also making some trips to Germany, France, Switzerland, Belgium, London and Scotland.

Their lives shared similar preoccupations and activities, such as reading, letter writing, enthusiasm for the ideas of The Enlightenment, the education of the poor, the abolition of slavery and lifelong devotion to a more conspicuous brother. In writing about them I have kept to the facts – where there are facts – but I have drawn on my imagination to respond to these two women's deep and lengthy lives. There are lots of gaps – this is not a biographical history. These poems are essentially a personal response to two remarkable women.

FEATHER AND BONE

EARLY

A wintry morning, drizzle on the pane,
your nose against the glass, misting the view.
Familiar shapes behind your eyes, the boys'
voices. And up ahead, the gurgling Derwent,
the dew-soaked grass – you're running full tilt
towards its laughter. You're with them now and
they are all around you, trying to catch
their Dorothy Mae but you are running
faster – back through years to being held –
you're nearly there, but then the arms
are swinging you round, lifting you up, right
over the ripples. And you can see quite
clearly now as you open your eyes
in Yorkshire, your mother's smile in the water.

DOROTHY'S COUNTRY

And if you go, go early
or better the night before,
beneath the moon's brim.

Step into well-worn shoes,
but step out the door a stranger,
leave all behind.

Sense in the birch's spine,
in each leaf exhaling, such light distilled –
let it flood your dull valley with colour.

Hear how a blackbird begins its own song
without trying. Try to unhinge who you are –
let it wing out your body;

let it pulse with each blade, each stone –
each solitary throb
that the moon is blessing.

Open it wide, the door between you
and out there, venture loose on the tide.
Let it carry you out of your depth:

imbibe this moment.

TAKEN

Already your plump little hands mimicked
hers, dipping in flour and loam,

clutching her skirts as she picked
sage and thyme from the garden.

A riot of children charging all day,
William already the difficult one –

your father's head deep in his desk,
all night the rushlight burning.

Was that why she went –
for a breather, a walk on the wild?

The lorn draper's daughter
lost between damp London sheets,

stopping the coughing-box coach
short of home,

short of breath
at her hapless parents'.

Knew she was leaving her half-lived life,
her lovely loud boys,

a little girl wary of bruising
a butterfly's wing.

Her breathless ask of Elizabeth –
Dear cousin, please care for my Dorothy.

What was it like, aged four, uprooted so quick,
transplanted to good Yorkshire soil?

Part of you thrived,
part of you never filled.

THE EMBRYO OF SONG

The soothing hover of single wren,
sonorous as that handful of feather and bone
he heard once as a boy

from the nave of Furness Abbey. Bodiless notes
soared free, cancelling thoughts
that pressed their dead weight home.

And though he walked away alone
that presence carried with him, a constant nesting
in his head, the embryo of song;

not yet knowing she would bless his path,
his page, his roof – 'a hidden Bird that sang'
the missing note for both of them.

'RAMBLING ABOUT THE COUNTRY ON FOOT'

My dear Aunt, I am twenty-three,
my face nut brown and no Place
dearer than here in step with my Brother –

closer than kin,
more than my stolen Mother, Father, Home,
we are part of each other.

So what if they stare,
this is the Bliss too long denied,
the Tenderness that never sleeps,

that fills something amiss,
redeeming his ache and mine
at every turn in the road,

in each Lake's mirror.

Dear Aunt –
you can't deny me this.

'SHE WHOM NOW I HAVE'

Out of a world half-starved she lurched
hungry for light,
keen eyed,
'a perfect electrometer'
walking this clutch of precious years,
attendant to his pacing out the words,
hands clasped behind his back.

Hers did the work, scribbling after –
her eyes, her ears, her heart in tow.
The two of them tied and feeding
some kind of fierce umbilicus,
bringing forth that wild, demanding
Lucy child of poetry.

No Boundary

The day you met him in Dorset
when Coleridge cleared the fence
and then the pond, a disarming figure

leaping light as a hare right up to you;
when he looked you in the eye,
that grey receiving eye, and then his voice –

a river from somewhere else you'd half-imagined
lifting you off the ground and taking you there –
he turned your head.

'At first I thought him very plain', you wrote to Mary,
but once he opened his mouth …
nothing else mattered.

The three of you talked through the night,
and you felt it then, the dull ache lift,
a soul half-lost, connecting.

The beginning so brimming;
no boundary would intervene,
no distance part your thoughts.

You'd tramp the lakes and fells,
the streets of Europe –
'a sett of violent democrats' for poetry.

But closer in, the thing that held –
you'd share the downward tread.
And when apart, you'd live for every letter.

Why did they fall out of rhyme?
Was it a matter of lyric
or disposition?

Better you couldn't tell
that walking the wilds together would wear
eventually like shoe leather

to halting disrepair.
You'd lose
that lovely river.

HOME

And when
he opened the door for you
five days before Christmas,
after the journey
    chill and mystical,
the damp calling out for kindling,
it was that moment
    all over again
of finding where you belonged:
a roof
        and a hearth
               and your brother.

My Dearest Coleridge

How things were then when I first penned
a letter to you from Grasmere.
Dorothy beside me racked with the ache,
a mountain of bed curtains
stacked for her thread and needle.

And how things are now.
The downstairs view is gone,
the door still opens to all who call –
now they come for crumbs of our lives, not bread.
The walls still hold, the chimney draws,
the burn of the coal-scuttle top of the stairs

still there – but we are nowhere.
All that remains of us is dust and ink.
And yet, in our words we still can move;
we still can move in words.

'LOW LIVING, HIGH THINKING'

Town End, frugal commune of lyrics,
porridge, debate and re-used tea.
De Quincey, Coleridge, Scott
all warmed to their theme
in the draw of Dorothy's fire.

A WAY OF LIFE

Drawn to kindred, half-lost souls, you listened
to them, wrote them into the landscape

that you walked and loved and breathed, keeping
old Fisher busy stitching leather.

Hoofed it to Ambleside and back, sometimes
by moonlight in hope of a letter.

Dried still-fragrant leaves for a second brew,
the third for the neighbours.

Speared as many stitches as words, shirt after shirt,
stocking after stocking.

Papered the walls with newsprint above the buttery
trying to line little lungs against the damp.

These were the patterns that cut and pinned your life.
For years the walking worked its balm,

the robin's slender song, the light on Rydal
letting you belong, for a while –

the wind in your weathering face,
the seeds of wild white foxglove wrapped

in a docken to take home and plant
in your mutual 'slip of mountain' at Town End.

DAYLIGHT ROBBERY

Hungrier for light than meat,
they scraped the pot to pay the tax –
two windows over the limit.
Six shillings to keep them unbricked,
they wouldn't be robbed of daylight.

When You were Low

Along the shore where you'd sat on a stone
bereft, resolved to write him a journal,

I met five bullocks in a roadside field;
horns no more than bumps; tails swatting flies

in the shade of an oak, their tearing pull
of the grass like the lake water lapping.

A granted ease in their solid bodies, their
handsome woolly heads, already accustomed

to traffic. The closest one gave me a stare;
peat-deep eyes, thick lashes and easy brow.

Weighing me up in one impassive look,
he breached the nettled hedge for something better –

pink flesh of tongue entwined sweet heckberry,
missing the barb by a stroke.

You met a blind man with two sticks when you were low
'driving a very large beautiful Bull and a cow'.

'A SHEEP CAME PLUNGING'

Frightened by an insignificant Dog
    on the other side,
a sheep came plunging up the Bank,
    passed close to us,
its fleece dripped a glittering shower
    under its belly.
Primroses by the roadside, pilewort
    shone like stars in the sun,
violets, strawberries retired and half-buried
    among the grass.
When we came to the foot of Brothers Water
    I left William.
Went right of the Lake through the wood.
    I was delighted –
the water under the boughs of the bare old trees,
    simplicity of the mountains,
the exquisite beauty of the path. And there,
    one grey cottage.
I repeated 'The Glow-worm' as I walked,
    hung over the gate
and thought: I could stay here forever.

DOMESTIC ARRANGEMENTS

Made use of the buttery's chill
as a store; a walk-in fridge without a door,
no controls, just a stone slab floor
with a stream bed below.
When it flooded food kept for longer.

POSTBAG

Stitch-work of fir trees:
firelight, night and pale moonlight thread.
Shelter for letters
bearing her words,
this time to her dearest brother.

Dull the return from the post –
empty as she is empty.
No answer to read by the moon
to shorten the journey home.
Her sky clouds over.

How will it fare when answers come
co-signed by William and Mary?
How will it carry as true
as the swallows' constant return
to the eaves above her window?

For a while the moon will dim.
She will begin
to notice the stars come and go,
will write what she feels
through her eyes, to fill her own missing.

For a while,
the bag will be nest
to her own wild,
fledgling notes
of poetry.

Making Light

Made their own candles
dipped in hot tallow,
layers of reeking wax
shedding light and smoke
in equal dose.

'EVERY QUESTION … THE SNAPPING OF A LITTLE THREAD
ABOUT MY HEART'

Has it happened to you?
Someone unwittingly grills you for news
when your world's in the balance of half-read words?

When you want to absorb them letter by letter
with only the moon looking over your shoulder,
only its cold, yellow stare?

Have you too closed your door
to sit in the dark with the kind of reply
neither heart nor hand can bear?

IN JOHN'S GROVE

The lake is a sheet of stillness –
    the day draws nearer.

The moon rises clear over Silver How,
my heart melts into its well of yellow reply –
    the day draws nearer.

Eyes closed beneath the firs,
the 'voice of the air' wraps round us –
    the day draws nearer.

You say you could die in this moment
I hold like my breath, as the firs lean over –
    nearer, nearer.

The lake is a sheet of stillness –
    the day draws nigh.

'The roses are fretted and battered and quite spoiled.
The honeysuckle, though in its glory, is sadly teased.
The peas are beaten down.
The scarlet beans want sticking.
The garden is overrun with weeds'.

'A Feeling of Something Being Amiss'

Did she lay it down by the water's fall,
beckoned by limbs of silver
into the brim of heather and no heather
purpling hill and pool –
    into the pull of it all.

Her voice off the page as rain off the road
releasing the earth's true tones
and rinsing them brighter.

Her urgent unravelling eye
diffusing heartache and headache
in realms of luminous cloud,
thoughts afloat
    and halfway adrift,

trusting the pitch of her craft, the feeling itself,
to the oars of water boatmen, the lull of Grasmere.

THE LITTLE HORSE

Smithed in Belgium, bargained for in France,
ferried from Calais, most likely on Dorothy's hand.

Her finger finds the hallmark's sign,
a tiny horse engraved outer side of the ring.
Admire it as she might,
this is the pledge intended for dear Mary.

Here the hooves, the canter, the steady back,
the sure-footed Fell, the well-natured hack,
the quick, clear eye, the responsive mouth,
the untamed mane, the deep-hearted girth.
No matter who the wearer, whatever the ground,
these hooves outside the ring would bring him home.

THE RING

All night you lay
within its circle
wondering.

He knocked and came in,
raised you up like a child from the bed,
withdrawing the ring from your finger;

impulsively slipped it back on,

blessing those hands again,
that body and soul of a sister
who'd saved him from going under.

What words exchanged before he went to her?

Through the pane you watched them alter,
her arm in his for the church
you would not enter.

Collapsed on your bed with the ache in your head,

how the bells tolled as you lay,
pealing away your life
with the ring of betrothal.

You would be three now.

'ON FRIDAY, 8TH, WE BAKED BREAD'

Two days home.
Two women in the kitchen.

Bread needs baking.
Dorothy stokes the fire,

Mary sprinkles flour on the table like snow,
does not remove her ring to pummel the dough
that Dorothy tips in a bowl and leaves to prove.

She walks out into the air and up the steep garden.
Mary stands beside her, watching a bee
in a foxglove the colour of snow,

that Dorothy says she transplanted from its home.

They knead the bread between their snow-floured hands,
shape it and while it bakes the table is scraped,
slates swept, aprons hung on a nail.

It comes out risen.
Dorothy cuts the heel,
they eat as they climb the path towards John's Grove

where light filters through the firs like flakes of snow
melting into the silent floor that holds them –
the lull of tender earth and proving air.

The sun grows strong, the clouds break blue
and they go on to drink the view of Rydale.

Later, Dorothy writes:
'The first walk that I had taken with my sister'.

WORDSWORTH'S BACK DOOR

I

Had a back door installed
to skip the domestic.
In from the garden,
halfway upstairs and calling.
Pacing the floor, perched
on his cutlass chair, or
up at the window, eyes
on the lake water, staring.
Mary or Dorothy lending
a seasoned hand, a keen ear;
taking each syllable down,
weighing, sifting, blending.

II

Why not? Your own way in
direct to that life upstairs where
an un-walled room is waiting –

but narrow no-one's field to get you there.
Imagine that door in the back of your life.
Turn the handle, swing the hinge:

all it takes
    – it takes all –
        to cross the threshold.

PITCH

When the cock bird commands the run of the pen,
crows for the whole of her eye;

when he repairs to the upper bough,
the hens attuned to his call;

when his plumage is much like theirs
remarkable though in reflecting light;

when we perceive how the hen house works
its synthesis of art –

doesn't it colour and clarify
what we hear in the song's full flight?

A Postscript for Dorothy

And how the moon might have cracked
and birthed anew,
filled with ink in whole eclipse
had you walked your own wild gait
instead of reining in to serve his rhyme.
Or might you never have taken a step
beyond the parsonage gate
without that certainty
instilled in him
by you?

'TRIFLING AS IT IS'

May this thimble of light
help mend tears,
pull fraying edges together.
May it gleam in the firelight,
outshine any ring.
May it be second skin
to your working finger.

'Trifling as it is',
put it on.
Let it be shield against arrows,
let it make stitches sure.
Whatever you stab in anger,
may you not draw your own blood.

DORA'S FIELD

So much in the undertow of roots
weaving here your silks of mist
and moss, of earth and clouded water.

So much wanted, so much warped by want.
So much depends on the roots,
the way they burrow and clamp to the hill

sending up tendrils of long-armed beech,
of stubborn oak, ignoble elder
cradling the field

for spring to come, ignite your hidden store,
your siphoned gold, perennially renewed –
a tongue-less riot of shaking daffodils.

They don't all dance, as Dorothy saw.
Some lay a heavy head on stone,
your too soon pillow.

Visiting Allan Bank

The charred beams, the undressed walls, the well-worn
welcoming floors keep Dorothy's fire stoked –

without the smoke that drove them out –
with all the reaching light that they let in.

Zoom in on squirrels, birds, a falling leaf,
or turn to another view: that crucial

little island almost sold – catalyst
that brought about the Trust beneath this roof.

Open any book in any room and feel
the ghosting words rise off the page, the brush

of thoughts against your lips, the watercolour
bleed of how things were, and still are here –

no virtuous re-creation intervenes.
A halfway house where past and present meet

in open door and outlook. Come, sit down
and read. Reflect, pore over maps or talk

across the table, raise a cup. Take all
the time you need, things are fluid here.

This benign 'abomination' of a house
is offering you space to think and breathe.

Silver Howe in June

That bird of prey up there in the clouds
that sweep the hill like a swarm of passing thoughts,

that buzzard that hangs in the sky
as if it always has and always will,

hears, keener than me,
the bleat of half-grown, half-lost lambs,
the swallows' restless call,
the business of bees failing,

and heavier than thunder,
our own electric hum,
the traffic's constant whine,

and punctual as death
the tearing asunder of heaven's cloth by military jets.

That bird of prey up there, hears, keener than me,
profoundly through it all, pure or polluted,

the trickle and roar, the lick and pour
of wind and rising water.

ON READING DOROTHY'S JOURNAL

It's down to you I see the sullen droop
of an uprooted cowslip, the shimmering
of the birch, her papery skin; take in

a man by the side of the road, the hang
of his neck, his shoulders; see that his face
is closed like a flower, light-sensitive.

And now I see how a mother ekes out
the beans and rice from the food bank; keeps
her children occupied with games;

see the weight on her back where hope
has hardened with debt, as she watches, waits
for them to grow sick of it and stray.

It's down to you I see the gorse blooms gold
again regardless, see the birch shines through,
how many kinds of hunger walk the road.

FOUND POEMS IN LATE LETTERS

1

'DEAR EDWARD, COUSIN'

A madman might as well try
to tell you his doings … as I unravel mine.
From where I lie, the light from the window
lights on my Doves in their cage,
they have one another.
Poor Mary Lamb has lost all
in losing her brother –
a solitary twig in the storm,
still enduring …

2

'MY DEAREST DORA'

My thoughts are wilderness,
news be my resting place.
Poor Peggy Benson rests in the Church-yard
beside her once beautiful mother.
Fanny Haigh is gone to better ...
My friend Mrs Rawson has ended her pilgrimage
at ninety and two, while I,
having fought and fretted and striven,
am still seated here by the fire.
My Doves behind me by the small window,
laburnum shivers its naked seed pods,
the pine trees rock from their base.
I cannot write more, so farewell.

Late

A wintry morning, drizzle on the pane.
Your nose against the glass, misting the view.
Familiar shapes behind your eyes, the boys'
voices. And up ahead, the gurgling river,
the dew-soaked grass – you're running full tilt
towards its laughter. You're with them now
and they are all around you, trying to catch
their Dorothy Mae, but you are running
faster – back through years to being held –
you're nearly there, but then the arms
are swinging you round, lifting you up, right
over the ripples. And you can see quite
clearly now as you open your eyes
in wilderness: your mother's smile in the water.

CONSUMPTIVE OR NOT –

From the house tall and straight
on the street with a bridge
crossing that riverbed heart,

their little sister on spindly legs
hopped and kept hopping over and back,
three times without stop.

Consumptive or not,
raised on plain fare and leavening words,
whatever her spirit sailed out on

this sister would not give up.

DAVID MANSON'S SCHOOLROOM

By your time it had moved from the entry:

an upstairs Eden down Donegall Street
fields and green air at the window
the master spreading out cards and maps –

the gates wide open.

There you sit, playing owners and tenants
of knowledge, heads together
on how to increase your yield.

Already, at ten, in your element

totting up numbers
taking each problem apart
to solve inequalities –

a mission to make things balance.

He calls you all by name, boys and girls,
shows how his latest invention works –
a spindle machine, his gift

for the girls in the Poorhouse.

You ask why they don't come to school
and the older ones laugh but don't answer.
You think of the skin-and-bone waifs

the clang of the tall iron gates,

the cry sometimes of a runaway
shut in the hole;
your mother's arm around you,

her voice with the women's voices
unburdening the basket.
And the weight of knowledge hangs

no longer light on your slim shoulders.

ROSEMARY STREET

The street remembers when it was a lane,
remembers the spark of her heels

on the cobblestones, and later the words
carved deep in a doorway:

'Faithful to the last'; mindful of the lamp oil
burning deeper into the night,

the scrape of nib on paper; the writing tightly
argued, cajoling, pressing the case

for human right – all in her slight,
unshakable hand, holding her own.

This place is crying out for her, waiting
for that quickening step again.

INTERNMENT
a piece of an Ash tree in his loft

Ashplant or pike staff under the eaves,
a pamphlet at your elbow by the loom –

all it takes to be herded
onto the tender out in the Lough

stalled,
stagnating in the heat,

breathing in each other's thoughts,
fear spreading and typhus.

Imagine the hills at sundown,
the fields on either side

plunging headlong,
ripening for the scythe.

With brother after brother marshalled south,
houses ransacked,
weavers on the run,
countrymen hung by the heels and spun,
whipped to unravelling,

in plainest light
the hand that balanced books tears up the sheet,
pays out a spidery thread
that gains its own momentum.
It is

entirely your hand slipping through the bars
to one who reads in that same light
beyond the ordered sentence
of the state, the church, the day
beyond unequal.

No more full stops to halt the flow,
no halfway measures now,
no easy way to skirt
the field or scaffold,
no airy tale.

'Let us not be terrified or dismayed,
but repose
with unlimited confidence
where we can never be deceived ...
truth must prevail'.

THE LIBERATING ART

It is late in the darkening house.

From a simmering well
the stroke of the quill
as it charts the pull of resistance

of unbound thought.

In the grace of the candle
you conjure
your own unsinkable craft

to cover the criminal distance from north to south.

Spluttering wax brings you back
to the table, the chair, these walls
this mooring of light.

It is late
about two in the morning,
bid god speed and goodnight.

'THE MODERATE MEN ARE SOUND ASLEEP'
– Dr William Drennan

Rest assured
a blinkered horse between the shafts
has greater vision

than us fair-minded middle-of-the-roaders,
sleepwalking our way past heads on spikes.
Have no fear –

we'll not be rearing up at the crack of a lash
on a woman's back, or gagging
as a body we know swings senseless.

Rest assured
a blinkered horse between the shafts
holds keener sense in daydreams

of open ground,
an unbarred mouth
re-membered freedom of movement.

SEARCH PARTY

Glorious summer mocks the deeds of men
scattered at Antrim, at Ballynahinch,
the green betrayed in blood.

Two women can bear it no longer.

Cotton frocks and straw bonnets,
baskets packed for a picnic
head down through streets where

all they hear are the floggings,
the lash and its answering cries
subduing their curfewed town.

Miles on foot out Whitehouse way
avoiding yeomen – cautiously door
to unlocked door along the lough.

One gleans news that her husband is safe –
but will not desert her sister's search
through field and ditch and bog.

Two women out in the open.

Their hems torn, footsore
in the wild, untrodden heather,
look up to the brow and there he is

with Hope on bleak Bohill.

YOUR TWENTY-EIGHTH, 8TH JULY 1798

One month after Antrim,
a weave of subterfuge,
spies and soldiers everywhere you look.

All your shuttling back and forth
to borrow, bribe, beg,
secure safe passage.

Your father asks a favour of a seadog:
the vessel poised
the north side of the Lough.

A stone's throw from the quay he's recognised –
a yeoman that once worked for him
sees through the labourer's garb, makes the arrest.

Heavy as Cavehill about your shoulders,
the gift of your brother
bound in Carrick Castle.

Knowing he will not spill,
will not betray his own,
you feel your knees give way.

ON

Knot the ribbon,
twin loops, not single.

Fingers find the tear in the veil
your sister stitched together
ripped by a guardsman's sword
in the throng

before
your brother rose to the occasion of his hanging,
accepted the rope like a garland round his neck.

An hour ago it seems

the heavy door feels heavier,
pause on the threshold
listening for something.

The same Rosemary Lane with sparrows cheeping
the world at its business,
nothing – everything – nothing

has altered.

Force your feet down the entry –
a harmless handcart
rattles right through you

stopping your breath as you see there again
in its splintered arms
the cooling corpse

that housed the lungs, dear head,
the heart
you could not waken.

Your own beats hard in its slender cage.
On you go
without flinching.

CAUGHT

In a downpour,
drops of morning bead the brim
of her bonnet,

darken its weave,
her sleeves, her dress,
as if she is bleeding.

This is her grief the rain is grieving.
Gathering her skirts she runs
through sorrow's stream.

As She Sits in Gloom

In the meeting house
in the broad, high-minded, one-way-facing
quiet of her childhood,
in the stilling of prayer,

the strain of wheels on the cobbles,
the weight of great hooves,
the cry of a child from the street
find her there,

impart their blessing.
Answer enough
in the standstill of her life

to pull her to her feet,
towards the natural light
pouring under the door.

CLAIMING HIS PLACE

Was that the hardest part,
drawing a line through his name?
Was it a salve to nestle yours below,
to take a familiar title from the shelf
and sit where he might have sat
in the light from the window,
open the well-thumbed page and find:

Reading furnishes the mind
only with materials of knowledge,
it is thinking that makes what we read ours.

Thinking only how he would have smiled
at eyebrows raised, the consternation caused
among the esteemed and staid
the day you expanded their ranks
in the hallowed reading room.

THAT 'COMELY SMILE'

And did it draw you in as well?
All the young ladies sizing him up,
how handsome, how manly, this librarian –
potential husband material, this
ideal Irishman with an unfinished script.
Or was it his eloquent tongue
that matched your vision?
What would you have given
to stand beside Thomas Russell,
Harry and Wolfe Tone on the ancient stone
of McArt's Fort, committing yourself
beyond creed, beyond nation?

Only on paper you truly corresponded
and even then, he cast your final letter
on the fire unread, to spare your head
when his would soon be severed.
You gave him burial, this man
whose heart belonged elsewhere.

ELLEN, SHE MIGHT HAVE SAID

It's time.
Put on your shawl and come.

She walked beside me into the street,
held my hand as we crossed Four Corners;
knocked the big door and smiled
as if we were friends, as if
we were sharing a secret.

A maid with a cap let us in,
the mistress eyed me straight and said:
You come on Miss McCracken's word –
don't let her down.
Work hard and we'll get on.

I didn't want to stay there on my own,
missed the others' talk,
familiar sounds and smells.
This house reeked rich as the room
at the top of the Poorhouse stairs.

I feared the mistress and her frown.
What if I stitched it wrong?
But I sat down at the table
under the skylight, turned
to the work before me and began.

It was easy.
I flew through the bits of mending.
Took my time with the girl's
lace bodice. Fancied it was
for May, my little sister.

The clock struck five
the mistress smiled

and there was Miss McCracken,
walking me back to the Poorhouse gates,
pressing something solid into my hand.

A silver thimble in my palm,
around its rim the letters of my name:
no one could say it was stolen.
I turned to thank her,
but she had hurried on.

RECONCILIATION SHEET

Reckoned the cost of every thing:
oxtail, oats, ham bones for soup,
strings for a harp, lodgings for Atty,
the cost of his sweets and music paper.

The cost of counting on neighbours,
of flour sacks, cambric, the coach to Dublin –
the cost of the lash on the backs of the horses
muslin in purest white for the gaoler's wife.

The lifelong gift of a sister's hand:
her craft – your figures, your running – her calm.
The cost of keeping going, supplying demand,
of feeding mouths – outspinners', weavers' kin.

The gain of open arms to take his Maria in;
the insurmountable price of a brother's life;
the grief not ending there, the loss ongoing.
You drew a line through pity, knew the score

of the quill; embarrassed committees beyond
their natural mean, realised in soap and sheets
and lime the right to be clean in the bowels
of charity, behind those stately walls.

Ninety six years you kept on,
reconciling loss to incremental gain.

JUST

And did you sometimes want to cast it aside,
pack it back in the box,
return it there, where your mother's milliner's hands
picked the first one out for you?

Just to be
back up Cavehill on horseback,
Harry beside you, debating the *Rights of Woman*,
listening, lamenting, laying down the law.
Your big visions drawing you on,
looking out on the Lough and Carrickfergus,
not knowing the way things would go –
just to throw your head back and laugh,
the Northerly wind in your hair and letting it blow.

No Rest

Though curvature had done its best
to curb her reach, she stood unbowed,

at 88 still walked the quay she'd walked
with those long gone;

accosted captains, merchants, passengers –
accosts us still to break the slaving chains that shackle
limbs
and minds:

be more than passengers
don't rest
for less than even.

Do not be deceived by the words inscribed.
Mind when they were penned,
how politic, how purblind
to narrow her to that heart-pour of tears
that cost her dear,
barred from the closing moments of his life –
the dying male,
the weeping female.
A frame of words completely missing out
her head, her hands
the years and years and years
she practised what he died for:
díleas go héag.

BIRCH AND HAW TREE

They started out secure in similar soil.

One, uprooted early, leaned to home
towards a certain light, grew sensitive
to rain, to every bird that sang among
her leaves, to insect wings and northern
winds and every fragile nesting.
A tree that bloomed her silvery best
within another's shadow.

The other stayed quite small
but tough, rebuffed prevailing winds,
and when her closest was cut down
wove her branches tight as hedge,
a hiding place, a shelter.
Feared as the haw left standing in the field,
she stood her thorny ground.

SHE WRITES

She writes to see things clear, to clear her head;
to hold the brittle moment in a line.
She writes about the living not the dead.

Is it for him alone that she draws breath?
The heady brew of bold, enquiring minds?
She writes to see things clear, to clear her head.

Daily she meets the ruined and unfed.
Outrage fuels her pen, and simple pain.
She writes about the living not the dead.

It bears her sense of self, this gathering thread
pulling her through each low and losing time –
she writes to see things clear, to clear her head.

She does not write for us, though we can tread
inside her words, falling in step to find
she writes to see things clear, to clear her head,
she writes about the living, not the dead.

BUT FOR THEIR DIPPING PENS

In truth,
they both preferred the tongue,
the swirl of words in the mouth,
their northern twang;
the to and fro
between friends – well water
shared on the road – a sojourner's story;
the surge of argument pounding on stubborn rock.

That said,
without the flow of thought crammed onto paper,
we'd never grasp that foxglove feel for things
from inside out, that Dorothy way
of seeing;
never trace the grit of Mary Ann working
away at the cracks, to let the light
break through on things kept dark.

But for their dipping pens,
we could not dip beneath the selfless surface,
could not begin to fathom how they held.

The Brimming View

Dorothy remembers a carpet of moss,
the flowers she was to plant with Coleridge
and her brother; the rock, the brimming view.

Mary Ann looks up from the greedy quay,
the din and rumour of the street
up to the constant hill.

Audible still to the inner ear
that airy bird –
the call they recognise,

crystallising song
in a surge of notes
delivered on the wing –

that unremarked trajectory their own,
the two of them feather and bone
with the soaring lark.

p. 15: In her fourth year, on the sudden death of her mother from pneumonia, Dorothy was sent to live with her mother's cousin Elisabeth in Yorkshire.

p. 17: This refers to an experience which William Wordsworth related. The wren could not be seen but its voice 'cancelled thoughts that kept pressing' (his own words) at a time when he had not found himself or poetry. In *Home at Grasmere*, part one of *The Recluse*, he refers to Dorothy as a 'hidden bird that sang', like that illusive wren, embedding her crucial role. The line here, 'And though he walked away alone' echoes a line in Louis MacNeice's poem, 'Autobiography'. Although the circumstances of each poet differed, there is perhaps a shared sense that poetry would emerge as the way forward.

p. 18: The title is taken from one of Mrs Crackenthorpe's letters (1795) to her niece, remonstrating about Dorothy's unladylike behaviour in undertaking a walking tour solely with her brother. The capitalised words in the body of the poem are drawn from Dorothy's letters to her childhood friend, Jane Pollard, as well as her Aunt.

p. 19: from *Home at Grasmere*, William Wordsworth. Coleridge likened Dorothy to a perfect electrometer, for her responsiveness in conversation. The electrometer was a new-fangled gadget that reacted to metals such as gold like a thermostat.

p. 20: 'At first I thought him very plain, [I wrote to Mary]': from a letter Dorothy W wrote to Mary Hutchinson (June, 1797), describing her first impressions of S T Coleridge.

p. 20: 'a sett of violent democrats': Coleridge, Wordsworth and their radical friends (Lamb, Hazlitt, Southey ...) were dubbed this by some of the villagers in Nether Stowey where Coleridge lived at the time.

p. 22: On 20 December 1799, five days before Dorothy's 28th birthday, the cottage which had previously been a tavern at Town End became hers and William's for £5 a year.

p. 24: 'Low living high thinking': William W's epithet for the régime at Town End.

p. 25: 'slender': Coleridge's description of a robin, quoted by Dorothy in her journal.

p. 25: William Wordsworth wrote to Coleridge on Christmas Eve 1799, 'she has already built a seat with a summer shed on the highest platform in this our little domestic slip of mountain'.

p. 27: Quote and setting refer to the first entry in Dorothy's *Grasmere Journal*, 14 May 1800, in which she 'resolved to write a journal of the time till W & J return [(William and his brother John] ... to give Wm Pleasure by it when he comes home again'.

p. 28: 'A sheep came plunging': a found poem, drawn from *The Grasmere Journal* entry, 16 April 1802

p. 32: 'every question ... the snapping of a little thread about my heart': title from *The Grasmere Journal* entry, 12 April 1802.

p. 33: 'the voice of the air': from *The Grasmere Journal*, 29 April 1802, John's Grove. Dorothy and William listen to the waterfalls – 'it was a sound of waters in the air'.

p. 34: found poem directly quoted from *The Grasmere Journal*, 7 July 1802.

p. 35: 'a feeling of something being amiss': from a letter from Dorothy to Mary in the summer of 1802. She was troubled with headaches and toothache and an *'uneasy sense* of *emptiness'* (as she described it to Dr Beddoes) throughout her life.

p. 38: 'On Friday 8th we baked Bread': from *The Grasmere Journal*, 8 October 1802 (sic quote in the last line).

p. 43: 'Trifling as it is': from a letter Dorothy wrote to her lifelong friend Jane Pollard.

p. 44: Dora's Field: planted with daffodils by William Wordsworth in memory of his daughter Dora, 1804–1847.

p. 45: Allan Bank was home to the Wordsworth family and friends for two years when Town End became too crowded. William called it 'an abomination' and they left largely because the chimney smoked so badly. Another famous resident was Canon Hardwicke Rawnsley, one of the founders of the National Trust. It was Grasmere itself and the proposed sale of the island in the middle of the lake which led to the creation of the National Trust.

p. 48: 'Dear Edward' and 'My Dearest Dora' are found poems drawn from two of Dorothy's late letters, to Dora Wordsworth, Spring 1838, and to Dorothy's cousin Edward.

p. 54: David Mansen was an inventor and brewer of beer as well as an innovative schoolmaster: *Every Tutor should endeavour to gain the affection and confidence of the children under his care ... and when punishment becomes necessary, should guard against passion and convince them 'tis not their persons but their faults which he dislikes ...*

p. 57: the quote is from a letter written by Mrs McTier in 1796 to her brother, Dr William Drennan.

p. 58: the closing quote is taken from one of Mary Ann's letters to her brother Harry (Henry Joy) held in Kilmainham Gaol.

p. 62: Henry Joy was sighted and arrested on Mary Ann's birthday, 28th July, the day she had arranged, through her father, free passage to America for her brother on the run.

p. 67: Quote from *Of the Conduct of the Understanding* by John Locke (1689). Mary Ann was permitted to take on her brother's membership of The Linen Hall Library after his execution.

p. 68: Mary Ann remarks on Thomas Russell's *comely smile* in a letter to a friend.

p. 71: The McCrackens, Mary in particular, gave bed and board to Edmund Burke (Atty) the harpist, supporting him in making an archive of Irish Harp Music. *his Maria* was the illegitmate daughter of Henry Joy. Against the wishes of her family, Mary Ann brought up Maria who looked after her aunt in old age.

p. 74: *díleas go héag*: true to the last, loyal unto death. Inscribed at Mary Ann McCracken's graveside.

ACKNOWLEDGEMENTS

Thanks are due to the editors of the following journals and books in which some of these poems or versions of them first appeared: *Four X Four*, *The Angry Manifesto*, *The Honest Ulsterman*, *Irish Pages*, *The Yellow Nib* and *Washing Windows? Irish Women Write Poetry* (Arlen House).

Thanks are also due to Natasha Cuddington for handprinting a limited edition of a version of the poem 'Pitch'.

I gratefully acknowledge the award of a writing bursary from the Arts Council of Northern Ireland and thank the staff of the Wordsworth Trust, the Linen Hall Library, Clifton House and Downpatrick Museum for their assistance.

Sincere thanks to Sheela Speers, Malcolm Scott, Robin Cameron, and Pamela Woof for reading early drafts. I am also grateful to artist Daniela Balmaverde for kind permission to use her artwork for the cover and to designer Joanne McCrum for her guidance. For the editorial support I have received from Arlen House, sincere thanks. And finally, thank you to all who gave me support and encouragement, in particular, my family, Word of Mouth Poetry Collective, Kate Brown, Geraldine Bradley, Damian Smyth and Moyra Donaldson.

Ruth Carr was born and lives in Belfast where she is a freelance editor and tutor. She was joint winner of the Maxwell House Bursary Award in 1981 and in 1985 edited *The Female Line* (Northern Ireland Women's Rights Movement, Belfast). She compiled the contemporary women's fiction section in *The Field Day Anthology of Irish Writing IV–V* (Cork University Press, 2001) and was a co-editor of *The Honest Ulsterman* for a number of years.

A founder member of the Word of Mouth women's poetry collective (1991–2016) her work is included in their anthologies, *Word of Mouth* (Blackstaff, 1998) and *When the Neva Rushes Backwards* (Lagan Press, 2014). Her poems have also appeared in various journals and anthologies including *Sleeping with Monsters* (Wolfhound, 1990); *The White Page* (Salmon Publishing, 1999), *A Conversation Piece* (Abbey Press, 2002); *The Blackbirds' Nest* (Queen's University, Belfast, 2006); *Our Shared Japan* (Dedalus, 2007); *The Natural History of Ulster* (Ulster Museums Northern Ireland, 2011), and *Washing Windows? Irish Women Write Poetry* (Arlen House, 2017).

She has two previous collections, *There is a House* (1999) and *The Airing Cupboard* (2008), both from Summer Palace Press. In 2015 she was a runner up in Mslexia's Annual Poetry Competition. She is co-organiser of an occasional reading series, *Of Mouth,* in the Linen Hall Library, Belfast.